Is It Alive?

By Diana Noonan

Pearson Australia
(a division of Pearson Australia Group Pty Ltd)
707 Collins Street, Melbourne, Victoria 3008
PO Box 23360, Melbourne, Victoria 8012
www.pearson.com.au

First published 2014 by Pearson Australia
2021 2020 2019 2018
10 9 8 7 6 5 4 3 2 1

Publisher: Sabine Bolick
Project Managers: Tamara Pirois and Rachel Davis
Lead Editor: Kerry Nagle
Editor: Anne McKenna
Series & Cover Designer: Jenny Grigg
Designers: Nina Heryanto and Adam McCrow
Copyright & Pictures Editor: Julia Weaver
Mac Operator: Rob Curulli
Printed in Australia by the SOS Print + Media Group

ISBN 978 1 4860 0763 9
Pearson Australia Group Pty Ltd ABN 40 004 245 943

Acknowledgements
We would like to thank the following for permission to reproduce copyright material. The following abbreviations are used in this list: t = top, b = bottom, l = left, r = right, c = centre.

Alamy Ltd: Tom Mackie, p. 13; Florilegius, p. 15r; AlphaAndOmega, p. 16.
Dreamstime: pp. 7, 9l, 10, 15l, 17, 20.
Fairfax Photo Sales: Justin McManus, p. 18.
Fotolia: p. 8.
Getty Images: De Agostini, p. cover; AFP, p. 5; Rodger Jackman, p. 12.
News Limited Images (Newspix): Romy Siegmann, p. 21; Chris Higgins, p. 22.
Pearson Asset Library: Peter Anderson (c) Dorling Kindersley, p. 6.
Shutterstock: pp. 1, 3, 4, 6, 9r, 10t, 11, 13, 14, 15, 19, 21, back cover.

Every effort has been made to trace and acknowledge copyright. However, should any infringement have occurred, the publishers tender their apologies and invite copyright owners to contact them.

Disclaimer
Some of the images used in *Is It Alive?* might have associations with deceased Indigenous Australians.
Please be aware that these images might cause sadness or distress in Aboriginal or Torres Strait Islander communities.

Contents

Living or non-living? 4

Is it alive? 6

How weird is that! 10

Extinction 14

The future – it's up to us 18

Connections 22

Glossary 23

Index 24

Living or non-living?

Our world is an amazing place filled with raging rivers and mighty mountains. It is a world of weird animals and wacky plants, towering skyscrapers and super-fast spacecraft. No wonder we say 'Wow!' at something every day.

Almost as amazing as the world itself is that every single thing in it fits into just two groups: living or non-living. Now that really is something to go 'Wow!' about!

This amazing insect looks just like a leaf.

LET'S FIND OUT

- **What do living things have in common?**
- **How different are living things from each other?**
- **What is extinction?**
- **How can we learn about living things that no longer exist?**
- **Why are living things still facing extinction?**

Living and non-living –
the difference is huge …

Is it alive?

Some living things look very similar to non-living things. So, how do you tell them apart?

Living stones

At first glance, this very strange plant is almost impossible to spot, especially if you're a sheep or a cow. The lithop, or 'living stone', is so good at hiding that if it had a brain, we'd say it was super-smart.

The lithop looks like the stones around it and its colour varies from shades of grey to orange and red. But the lithop is very different from real stones. That's because a lithop is a living thing and a stone is a non-living thing.

Stones or plants? Lithops look like the stones around them.

Stonefish blend in perfectly with their background.

Did you know?

Why pretend to be dead when you're actually alive? Some animals 'play dead' because keeping still protects them from **predators** that hunt moving creatures. Other animals, such as stonefish, pretend they're not a living thing at all, to help them catch prey!

A stone is never going to need food. Only living things need **nutrients** from food. The lithop gets its nutrients from the soil by drawing them up with its roots.

All living things need water, and the lithop's roots also draw up moisture from the soil. A stone will never need water, and it won't need air. Plants need air to provide them with a gas called carbon dioxide. Mixed together with nutrients and water, and the Sun's energy, this gas helps plants to grow.

Hiding among the stones with its **camouflage colours**, the lithop is fairly safe from other living things. But there's just one problem. While a stone doesn't need to reproduce (it will never produce a baby, an egg or seeds), a plant does.

The stones around the lithop will barely change at all, even over hundreds of years. But, every so often, the lithop takes a very important risk by leaving behind its camouflage protection. In order to produce seed, it flowers, and suddenly … the lithop doesn't look like a stone at all!

The lithop is easier to spot when it is flowering.

A racehorse is a living thing.

A bicycle is a non-living thing.

It moves, but is it alive?

Living and non-living things are different from each other, but they can share some **characteristics**. A horse (a living thing) and a bicycle (a non-living thing) can both move quickly. A racehorse can travel at 50 km/h. A racing bicycle can travel at more than 100 km/h! They can both travel long distances if they are well cared for – but this is where things become very different.

The horse needs food and water to move and repair its body. The bicycle needs oil and perhaps some new tyres. But a bicycle needs a living thing to make it move. That living thing is a rider, who needs to eat and drink.

How weird is that!

All living things have similar characteristics. Some show these in surprising ways, especially when it comes to finding food.

Plants that eat animals

While most plants use their roots to take in nutrients from the soil, others collect their food by behaving more like animals.

In places where plants can't get enough nutrients from the soil to survive, they catch small animals! Using juices that are a little like those in your own stomach, the plants turn their prey into a **liquid** that they can take in.

These Venus flytrap leaves are open, waiting to catch insects.

Did you know?

Earthworms have no nose! They do have a mouth, but they don't breathe through it. An earthworm gets **oxygen** by taking air into its body through its skin.

Finger-like cilia on the Venus flytrap's leaves trap the insect.

The Venus flytrap grows leaves with tiny hairs on them. These leaves can open and shut. When an insect lands on the hairs, the leaves snap shut. Tiny fingers, called cilia, on the edge of the leaves act like bars to stop the insect getting away.

It takes between 5 and 12 days for a Venus flytrap to **digest** an insect. If the flytrap's leaves snap shut on something that is not food (such as a pebble), the leaves reopen within 12 hours and throw the object out.

Venus flytraps come from North America. When kept as a pot plant in a home, they need only one or two insects a month to stay healthy.

Stomachs on the move

All living things need food to give them energy. Some animals swallow their food whole. Others chew their food into small pieces, ready to digest. But the sea star has a very different way of taking food into its body.

The sea star's mouth is on the underside of its body. If it finds prey too big to fit into its mouth, it will take its stomach to the food. To do this, the sea star pushes its stomach outside its body and uses it to surround its food with special chemicals called **enzymes**. These enzymes turn the food to mush, which the sea star then soaks up.

A sea star's stomach can work outside its body.

A sea star can push its stomach into a shell to eat the shellfish inside.

The sea star's special stomach-trick is also useful when it comes to getting to food in hard-to-reach places.

When the sea star finds a shellfish, it uses the strong **suction cups** on the underside of its arms to force open the shell just a crack. It pushes its stomach into the crack and surrounds what's inside the shell with enzymes. This turns the shellfish into mush, which the sea star sucks into its body.

Extinction

Extinction is a frightening word. It means that a whole **species** is no longer alive and there is no known way of bringing it back.

Missing – never to return

Scientists estimate that 90 per cent of all the animals that have ever lived on Earth are extinct. Some disappeared millions of years ago. Some will disappear in your lifetime.

When a species is found to be close to extinction, it is sometimes cared for in special places such as zoos and wildlife parks. It is hoped that its population will survive and increase.

Pandas raised in **captivity** are helping the species to survive.

Did you know?

Scientists estimate that only 10 per cent of plants and animals living today have been discovered.

A woolly mammoth

A giant moa

Fascinating, but gone forever

Dinosaurs, woolly mammoths and sabre-toothed tigers are some of the most fascinating animals ever to have lived, but they are now extinct. Some extinct living things, such as the dinosaurs, disappeared millions of years ago, and only their **fossils** remain. Others, such as the woolly mammoth, became extinct fewer than 4000 years ago, and pieces of their skin and hair have been found.

Just a few hundred years ago, a flightless bird called the giant moa lived in New Zealand. It weighed more than 200 kg and was almost 3 m tall. The bird was hunted to extinction. Pieces of its skin and feathers have been found, as well as its bones and eggs.

Hey, is that a dinosaur over there?

Hidden in rocks, bogs, **glaciers**, deserts and caves are the remains of living things that are now extinct. Sometimes people go looking for these animal and plant remains, digging their way into rock and earth, hunting for fossils. Just a few years ago, two people discovered the remains of a dicynodont as they were walking along a Tasmanian beach.

The dicynodont, an animal that lived 30 million years before the dinosaurs, was the first of its kind to be found in Australia. So it's always a good idea to watch where you're walking!

A model of a dicynodont

Perhaps volcanoes caused the dinosaurs to disappear.

What happened?

Extinction happens for many reasons. A **habitat** may become polluted. Plants and animals may be hunted until there are no more of the species left. But the reasons for extinction may also come from deep beneath the Earth or from space.

Dinosaurs disappeared more than two million years ago. Some researchers believe that **asteroids** in space collided with Earth. They think this created huge dust clouds that blocked the Sun and changed the Earth's climate. Others believe that the dust clouds were caused by volcanoes. The biggest mystery of all is that no one knows for sure why the dinosaurs became extinct.

The future – it's up to us

Human beings **dominate** the Earth, not in number, but in the way we change the planet. Sometimes we do it because of greed, sometimes we do it simply to survive.

Stop the bulldozers, save the trees

In some parts of the world where people are too poor to have electricity, they gather the few trees around them to use as firewood. This means these areas are losing their trees and are becoming deserts.

On a much larger scale, many of the world's rainforests are being cleared by bulldozers to make way for farming and mining. Some people believe that rainforests could disappear within 40 years. But many people are working hard to find solutions to save important environments.

Did you know?
Experts estimate that tens of thousands of species are becoming extinct each year.

Rainforest **logging** is responsible for the extinction of many species.

Pollution from factories sends harmful gases into the air.

Climate – control or catastrophe

Planet Earth is the perfect place for living things – at least it used to be. Now, scientists believe that Earth is becoming too warm. Huge areas of ice are melting. Low-lying countries may soon be in danger of flooding. Plant and animal habitats are changing and most scientists believe human beings are the cause of the problem.

Clogged with pollution and harmful gases, the Earth's **atmosphere** is trapping too much of the Sun's heat and our planet is becoming dangerously warm. Fortunately, many people think there is still time to change the way we live so that Earth remains a safe place.

Working towards a better future

If the future of our planet is to improve, it's up to humans – and that's us! Coal and oil give us energy that warms up the world too much. We need to find smarter ways to supply what people need.

Energy **generated** by the Sun, wind and water is safer for the environment. But this energy costs more to make and buy. Helping those who are too poor to use these forms of energy is essential. Re-using, recycling and simply using fewer resources is something we can all do to help stop the climate from getting warmer.

Wind-generated power may be better for the planet.

One way to help our planet is to plant more trees.

Learning to look after the planet

Some people don't know that our planet and many of the plants and animals living on it are in danger. Others know, but either don't care or are not sure what they can do about it. It is only by learning about how the world works that we can understand how to look after the place we call home.

Some of the best-known organisations working to teach people about how to care for the planet are the World Wide Fund for Nature and Friends of the Earth. There are many others and, thanks to tools such as the Internet, almost everyone can find out about them.

Connections

Everyone likes to think they can take care of themselves. The fact is, to remain safe and healthy, we all depend on each other and the environment we live in.

If we take care of living and non-living things, the Earth will not only be a safe place to live, its 'health' will improve. How will you help to make a difference?

It is important to help care for the planet.

Glossary

asteroids rocks orbiting the Sun

atmosphere the air around us

camouflage colours colours that help a plant or animal blend into its background

captivity unable to escape; animals in zoos and wildlife parks are said to be held in captivity

characteristics features or qualities that something has – what it looks and acts like

digest to break food down so the plant or animal can use it

dominate rule or control

enzymes a type of chemical

extinction when no member of a species is still alive

fossils the preserved remains of a living thing from the past (often found in rock)

generated created

glaciers very large areas of ice that move slowly

habitat the natural environment of a living thing

liquid a substance that flows like water

logging cutting down trees to use for timber and other purposes

nutrients the things a living thing needs to help it grow and repair itself

oxygen a gas that is part of air; living things need oxygen to survive

predators animals that hunt and eat other animals

species a group of living things with very similar characteristics

suction cups flat, round cups that stick strongly to another surface

Index

A
asteroids 17

B
bicycle 9

C
camouflage 8
carbon dioxide 7
climate 17, 19, 20

D
dinosaurs 15–17

E
earthworms 10
enzymes 12, 13
extinction 4, 14–18

F
fossils 15, 16

G
giant moa 15

L
lithop (living stone) 6–8

N
nutrients 7, 10

P
pandas 14
pollution 19

R
racehorse 9
rainforests 18
recycling 20

S
sea star 12–13
stonefish 7

V
Venus flytrap 10–11
volcanoes 17

W
woolly mammoths 15